How Communicate Jesus Effectively

Share Your GOOD NEWS!

Rev. Al Stewart, D.D.

Foreword by: Pastor Troy Warner

PoBoy Publishing © 2019

POBOY PUBLISHING

International Copyright Secured   Printed in the United States   Library of Congress IBSN: 9781090891907   All rights reserved.

Special thanks to my dear friend Abby Meyers of Lynchburg for her hard work and dedication in editing this manuscript.

Table of Contents

Foreword

How to Communicate Jesus Effectively
discusses a subject that most definitely
deserves to be highlighted today. Most
evangelicals either believe or have been
taught to boldly share their faith.
Additionally, most would agree they
should be sharing the good news of
Jesus Christ with the world around them
but fear, busyness and many other
things keep us from walking out this
clear mandate from Jesus to make Him
known. Al Stewart is a man uniquely
gifted to speak on this topic simply
because he shares the gospel. Everyone
who knows Al would quickly testify that
he is a faithful witness of Jesus Christ.
From doorsteps to friendships, Al is
intentional about sharing his faith in
Christ with everyone he encounters. It
is Al's in-the- trenches, every day
experience of evangelism that qualify Al

to help anyone who desires to be more effective in sharing the gospel.

In the pages that follow the reader will find no lack of Scripture or real-life examples for the witnessing situation. The exhortation given to share our faith is met with hands on advice that will prove helpful to those want to share their faith. As a well-studied Pastor, Al begins with Jesus as the best example, and then navigates the common land mines encountered while witnessing. This quick read will offer you key Scriptures to memorize and tools to equip you to get out there and share your faith.

Troy Warner,

Pastor of Calvary Chapel Lynchburg

Introduction

This is a book that I pray will serve as a practical guide to help everyone who reads this to reach others for Christ **MORE** effectively than you ever have. I make no special claim to having any *"patent"* on sharing Jesus, in fact as Dr. Leighton Ford *(Billy Graham's brother in law)* states concerning sharing the Gospel in his outstanding book on Evangelism *"Good News is for Sharing"* David C. Cook Publishing, 1977 on page 119: **"there are no surefire gimmicks or techniques."** When it comes to reaching others for Christ, I fully concur with Dr. Ford! There simply are no set formulas or *"canned"* approaches, etc., there are only insights each of us can give from our life experiences of being in the *"trenches"*. And of course the greatest example we will ever have is the Lord Jesus Christ Himself and remember this fact, He didn't win everyone he spoke to, in fact His success rate *(number's wise)* proves to us that we should **NEVER** judge our efforts by how many respond, after all can we really put a price tag on even one soul? *(You'll hear that phrase more than once in this book)* I'll devote the first chapter to how Jesus shared the truth of God's word as I mentioned He is and will always be our best example. And of course, He didn't win them all. In fact in the 6th chapter of John's account of the Gospel it came to a place where almost everyone abandoned Him! And speaking of Jesus and the situations He was often in, while I am certainly not Him, I to have been in the trenches for many, many years. So feel free to glean from this book all the things that will help you become a better and more effective communicator of the Good News of Jesus Christ to a very lost and broken world, and may I add, a very lost and spiritually broken United States of America, land that we love. Last, as with any book, I suggest you *"chew on the meat and spit out the bones"*.

Take what works and resonates within your heart and soul and don't worry about the rest; I don't expect anyone to agree with everything I say here. I can only share from my many years of experience in dealing with all types of people from all walks of life, from Presidents of companies to local Farmers working out in their fields. It's been a life I wouldn't trade for anything else and the best part is that as of this writing, it still continues, for Jesus said this in John 9:4 (HCSB) *We must do the works of him who sent me while it is day. Night is coming when no one can work.* This is a clear reference that this work of winning people to Jesus is for the *"here and now"* in this life, so each of us needs to make it count, me first!

In Christ,

Rev. Al Stewart,   3/15/19, 2:40 pm

Chapter 1

Jesus as our best Example

I guess you can say the title of this chapter goes without saying, but there is a very important fact that goes hand in hand with this statement, one that has given me great peace in my evangelistic ministry over these many, many years and that's this: despite being the very one and only Son of Almighty God, God among us Immanuel, Jesus did not win all He spoke to, in fact as I pointed out in the introduction, He was given a hard time by many and one would think with His final pronouncement to the World being His death on a cross that maybe He wouldn't be the best example? Many think that Jesus somehow failed by dying, but to those of us who know and understanding the power of His death which lead to His miraculous resurrection, His death became our life! This *"God-Man"* who walked the Earth like you and I, spoke and has become as so many have attested, even those who did not come to believe in Him, that He was indeed the greatest example our world has ever known or seen. So let's take an in depth look at why He is considered our model for Evangelism. What truths can we glean that we can use in our own approach in sharing His life with others, in fact did Jesus leave us such clues and insights as to how we can communicate God's *"Good news"* in a more effective fashion? I believe friends He did leave us clues and insights, in fact many as we will soon see!

- **Jesus and the Samaritan Woman**

John 4:1-15 (HCSB) *When Jesus knew that the Pharisees heard He was making and baptizing more disciples than John 2 (though Jesus Himself was not baptizing, but His disciples were), 3 He left Judea and went again to Galilee. 4*

He had to travel through Samaria, 5 so He came to a town of Samaria called Sychar near the property that Jacob had given his son Joseph. 6 Jacob's well was there, and Jesus, worn out from His journey, sat down at the well. It was about six in the evening. 7 A woman of Samaria came to draw water. "Give Me a drink," Jesus said to her, 8 for His disciples had gone into town to buy food. 9 "How is it that You, a Jew, ask for a drink from me, a Samaritan woman?" she asked Him. For Jews do not associate with Samaritans. 10 Jesus answered, "If you knew the gift of God, and who is saying to you, 'Give Me a drink,' you would ask Him, and He would give you living water." 11 "Sir," said the woman, "You don't even have a bucket, and the well is deep. So where do You get this 'living water'? 12 You aren't greater than our father Jacob, are You? He gave us the well and drank from it himself, as did his sons and livestock." 13 Jesus said, "Everyone who drinks from this water will get thirsty again. 14 But whoever drinks from the water that I will give him will never get thirsty again—ever! In fact, the water I will give him will become a well of water springing up within him for eternal life." 15 "Sir," the woman said to Him, "give me this water so I won't get thirsty and come here to draw water."

I'll stop here at verse 15, but Jesus goes on to give her a prophetic word about having had 5 husbands, then Jesus speaks of true worshipers being those who will worship *"in spirit and in truth"* and last, He confesses to her that He is indeed the long awaited Messiah. So what can we glean from Jesus words and actions here?

- **God loves without preference!**

  The contempt the Jewish people had for the Samaritans is well documented in History. They were *"half breeds and ignorant people"* to the Jews and many of them *(not all)* would go so far as to walk around Samaria to avoid any contact with them: *"One [main road] led...from Jerusalem past Bethany to Jericho, then north up the Jordan Valley and the west side of the Sea of Galilee toward Capernaum. To avoid Samaria, whose inhabitants the Jews despised, Jews often traveled this road in going between Galilee and Judea". (A Survey of the New Testament. Grand Rapids: Zondervan, 2012, p. 47).* So the first lesson we learn from Jesus is that in our witnessing opportunities we must **NEVER** ever be partial! Do not treat someone who looks or even smells better than another with more favor or who may have more *(financially, etc.)* this should never be the case friends!

- **Men and Women in Jesus Eyes**

That passage of Scriptures goes on to state this in verse 27: *"Just then His disciples arrived, and they were **amazed that He was talking with a woman.** Yet no one said, "What do You want?" or "Why are You talking with her?"* So why were they amazed? A Franciscan Media guest author wrote an article entitled *"Jesus extraordinary treatment of Women"* The guest author writes the following: *"A woman's place was thought to be in the home. Women were responsible for bearing the children, rearing them and maintaining a hospitable home. Men were not to greet women in public. Some Jewish writers of Jesus' time, such as Philo, taught that women should never leave the home except to go to the synagogue. Generally marrying* *young, a woman was almost always under the protection and authority of a man: her father, her husband or a male relative of her husband if she was a widow. This left women in a very vulnerable position within Judaism. They had little access to property or inheritance, except through a male relative. Any money a woman earned belonged to her husband. Men could legally divorce a woman for almost any reason, simply by handing her a writ of divorce. A woman, however, could not divorce her husband. In the area of religious practice, women were in many ways overlooked. Men were required to pray certain prayers daily, but women were not. While the study of Scripture was regarded as extremely important for men, women were not allowed to study the sacred texts. Rabbi Eliezer, a first-century teacher, is noted for saying, "Rather should the word of the Torah be burned than entrusted to a woman." At the Temple in Jerusalem, women were restricted to an outer court. In synagogues they were separated from the men and not permitted to read aloud. They were not allowed to bear witness in a religious court. But Jesus defies these expectations in at least three ways, which have implications for us.*

1) Jesus speaks with women in public

2) Jesus shows women respect and compassion

3) Jesus uses women Disciples

We should learn and glean from this that there is no room for chauvinistic behavior in our outreach opportunities,

Jesus makes it crystal clear that God is inserted in seeing **BOTH** men and women come to know Him in a real and personal way that He might use them!

- **Listen if God whispers to you**

Friend are you a Christian who is open to listening to what God is saying to you even while you are sharing His Good news with another? I am a Christian who boldly believes in Hebrews 13:8, that Jesus really is the same yesterday, today and forever. Therefore, what He did then, He can do today and forever period! Jesus spoke in a prophetic way to the Samaritan women, in the same manner God can whisper a truth to you about that person you are in front of, and when He does; do not be afraid to speak what the Lord gives you. Now this has happened to me so many times over all these years that I really don't know where to start…….. But I'll share with you this story that happened about 4 years ago, around 2015. I was with a new partner, a fine young man named Ryan when we came upon about the 3rd or 4th door of the day and this was his first time out with me in the field, a women answered the door and I saw a few children there and we began to talk and suddenly I am hearing the Spirit speaking to me saying *"this women feels totally defeated and on top of that, she has a tremendous gift I have given her, you must encourage her!"* WOW, what do I do with that? So with little hesitation *(I have come to a place of just knowing when the Lord is speaking to me)* that I began to share what I heard and in no time the tears ran down her face, in fact when I got to the part of asking her what this gift was, she just reached her hands to her necklace which featured a small microphone and being a musician myself I got excited and said *"you're a singer!"* In short, the entire word was right on, she was in the middle of a divorce *(one she needed to advance I might add)* and was just kind of drifting a bit. Well I invited her to our Church where I was Pastor at the time and a few weeks later had her sing and the Congregation was like *"wow"…..* She eventually came with my wife and I to help us start our present Church and while she travels around singing now, she is always glad to come back *'home"* and sing for us at Greater Grace Chapel. *(GGC)* God really is good and He really does care and we can fully trust Him.

- ## Jesus and the Rich Young Ruler

Luke 18:18-23 (HCSB) *A ruler asked Him, "Good Teacher, what must I do to inherit eternal life?" 19 "Why do you call Me good?" Jesus asked him. "No one is good but One—God. 20 You know the commandments: Do not commit adultery; do not murder; do not steal; do not bear false witness; honor your father and mother." 21 "I have kept all these from my youth," he said. 22 When Jesus heard this, He told him, "You still lack one thing: Sell all that you have and distribute it to the poor, and you will have treasure in heaven. Then come, follow Me." 23 After he heard this, he became extremely sad, because he was very rich.*

What truths can we glean from this exchange between Jesus and a young wealthy ruler?

- **Jesus didn't win them all!**

I have mentioned this a few times already in this book, but it is worth repeating, the fact that Jesus didn't win everyone He spoke to should actually give you and I realistic expectations in our efforts to reach others. Do not place undue pressure on yourself and if you go out one day and get no response back, trust me, that's totally okay! I truly believe that the God of the Bible is not a *"results oriented"* God, if He was, He probably would have written His name in the sky for the entire world to see and He certainly wouldn't have chosen the cross! Remember this, the Bible tells us clearly in 1 Corinthians 1:18 (HCSB) *"For the message of the cross is foolishness to those who are perishing, but it is God's power to us who are being saved."* So it's okay if you are not seeing immediate fruit for your efforts, stay tough and keep plowing, eventually you will see a few people come around, I know this to be true from experience.

- **Jesus must be our 1st priority**

A clear lesson here is that nothing should ever come before our relationship with the Savior. The sad fact here is that when Jesus challenged this man with what's most important in his life by telling him to sell all he had and follow Him, he was unable to do so. I think Matthew 6:33 clearly applies in a big way here: *"But seek first the kingdom of God and His righteousness, and all these things will be provided for you".* Simply put, when we make 1st

priority the Kingdom of God, then all else falls into place as it should. Had this wealthy young ruler agreed to sell his fortune, he would have gained the Savior and would have been rich in a way that his fortune could never have brought him!

- **Jesus words on outreach**

John 4:35 (HCSB) *"Don't you say, 'There are still four more months, then comes the harvest'? Listen [to what] I'm telling you: Open your eyes and look at the fields, for they are ready for harvest.* Notice what Jesus states here vs. what we think about the *"harvest."* *(The lost)* We say wait, but Jesus says they are ready now! Jesus words makes me think of one of my 25 passages you will read later for memorization. 2 Corinthians 6:2 (HCSB) *For He says: I heard you in an acceptable time, and I helped you in the day of salvation. Look, now is the acceptable time; now is the day of salvation.* **NOW** is the time, today is the day of salvation. Never put off to tomorrow what you can do today! *(Make sure you are hearing the Lord if you do!)*

Luke 10:2 (HCSB) *He told them: "The harvest is abundant, but the workers are few. Therefore, pray to the Lord of the harvest to send out workers into His harvest.* We are told by the Lord Himself that the harvest is abundant! In other words, there are always plenty of people to reach, that's never the problem friends. The problem is the lack of willing participants sadly. But thankfully we are given a solution, pray and ask the Lord to send out more workers. Will you join me in doing exactly that?

Luke 9:1-6 (HCSB) *Summoning the Twelve, He gave them power and authority over all the demons, and [power] to heal diseases. 2 Then He sent them to proclaim the kingdom of God and to heal the sick. 3 "Take nothing for the road," He told them, "no walking stick, no traveling bag, no bread, no money; and don't take an extra shirt. 4 Whatever house you enter, stay there and leave from there. 5 If they do not welcome you, when you leave that town, shake off the dust from your feet as a testimony against them." 6 So they went out and traveled from village to village, proclaiming the good news and healing everywhere.* Talk about receiving marching orders, here they are friends! So these 3 passages should be enough to convince each and every one of us of the importance of sharing Christ with others. And last Jesus spoke of a place that unbelievers will go; it is a place that the Bible calls Hell. *(Hades-Greek)* The words Jesus spoke concerning the rich man and Lazarus should send a chill up our spines in Luke 16. Luke 16:19-31 (HCSB) *"There was a rich man who would dress in purple and fine linen, feasting lavishly every day. 20 But a poor man named Lazarus, covered with sores, was left at his gate.*

21 He longed to be filled with what fell from the rich man's table, but instead the dogs would come and lick his sores. 22 One day the poor man died and was carried away by the angels to Abraham's side. The rich man also died and was buried. 23 And being in torment in Hades, he looked up and saw Abraham a long way off, with Lazarus at his side. 24 'Father Abraham!' he called out, 'Have mercy on me and send Lazarus to dip the tip of his finger in water and cool my tongue, because I am in agony in this flame!' 25 "'Son,' Abraham said, 'remember that during your life you received your good things, just as Lazarus received bad things, but now he is comforted here, while you are in agony. 26 Besides all this, a great chasm has been fixed between us and you, so that those who want to pass over from here to you cannot; neither can those from there cross over to us.' 27 "'Father,' he said, 'then I beg you to send him to my father's house— 28 because I have five brothers—to warn them, so they won't also come to this place of torment.' 29 "But Abraham said, 'They have Moses and the prophets; they should listen to them.' 30 "'No, father Abraham,' he said. 'But if someone from the dead goes to them, they will repent.' 31 "But he told him, 'If they don't listen to Moses and the prophets, they will not be persuaded if someone rises from the dead." Hell is a very real place! Jesus spoke about it clearly. This story strongly illustrates it. And Jesus words here lends credence to what Jude stated in his brief letter in Jude 1:20-23 (HCSB) *20 But you, dear friends, as you build yourselves up in your most holy faith and pray in the Holy Spirit, 21 keep yourselves in the love of God, expecting the mercy of our Lord Jesus Christ for eternal life. 22 Have mercy on those who doubt; 23 save others by snatching [them] from the fire; have mercy on others but with fear, hating even the garment defiled by the flesh.* Notice the term *"snatching theme from the fire"*. Do you feel, or can you see the urgency friends? Time is very limited and we don't have a lot of it in this life. James made that clear when he stated this in James 4:13-15 (HCSB) *13 Come now, you who say, "Today or tomorrow we will travel to such and such a city and spend a year there and do business and make a profit." 14 You don't even know what tomorrow will bring—what your life will be! For you are [like] smoke that appears for a little while, and then vanishes. 15 Instead, you should say, "If the Lord wills, we will live and do this or that."* So please join me in making the most of every moment God gives us. Don't hesitate to talk to family members, friends or strangers. I can assure you that your efforts will be rewarded by the Spirit of God showing up in a huge way!

Chapter 2

God Uses People!

So Many people I have talked to over the years seem to be waiting for that preverbal lightning bolt from God that in most cases never ever comes instead of stepping out and being obedient to the command of the Gospel to GO. *(Matthew 28:19)* I am sometimes befuddled by the statistics I read by groups like Barna and others which tell us that something like only one person in ten will ever lead another to Christ in their lifetime. How strange that is considering this fact, Jesus has already issued us *"marching orders"* if you will! And we end up practically ignoring those orders due to things like apathy, laziness or perhaps because we like sitting and staying in our ever dangerous *"comfort zones"*. So here are a few passages that contain these important marching orders: Luke 10:1-2 (HCSB) *"After this, the Lord appointed*

70 others, and He sent them ahead of Him in pairs to every town and place where He Himself was about to go. 2 He told them: **The harvest is abundant, but the workers are few.** *Therefore, pray to the Lord of the harvest to send out workers into His harvest".* We see here that Jesus has already told us that the harvest or the people are abundant or plentiful meaning there will always be enough people to talk to! That's never been the problem, the problem is the latter portion of this verse, and it's the workers as they are few. I am reminded of the Prophet Ezekiel when he received the Word of the Lord over the House of Israel and it wasn't a good one. It ended in verse 30 with this sad proclamation: Ezekiel 22:30 (HCSB) *"I searched for a man among them who would repair the wall and stand in the gap before Me on behalf of the land so that I might not destroy it,* **but I found no one".** Another Old Testament passage comes to mind where the Psalmist states in

Psalm 66:16-17 (HCSB) *"Come and listen, all who fear God, and **I will tell** what He has done for me. 17 I cried out to Him with my mouth, and praise was on my tongue"*. Jesus spoke these powerful words regarding the timing of the harvest: John 4:35-36 (HCSB) *"Don't you say, 'There are still four more months, then comes the harvest'? Listen /to what/ I'm telling you: Open your eyes and look at the fields, for they are **ready for harvest**. 36 The reaper is **already** receiving pay and gathering fruit for eternal life, so the sower and reaper can rejoice together"*. And perhaps the strongest evidence we have that God has entrusted us with His Holy Word for the purpose of imparting this truth to others is what the Apostle Paul wrote to his protégé Timothy: 2 Timothy 2:1-2 (HCSB) *"You, therefore, my son, be strong in the grace that is in Christ Jesus. 2 And what you have heard from me in the presence of many witnesses,*

commit to faithful men who will be able to teach others also".

This passage has always reminded me of the popular recycling logo which looks like this:

Can you see it? The Gospel goes from one to another, to another, to another and so on and so forth. Basically it's a never ending telling and reaching of others for Jesus Christ. So these are our marching orders friends. Jesus has made it undeniably clear that God in His infinite wisdom and plan from before time began entrusted mankind knowing he would be given the responsibility of carrying this message of reconciliation to all peoples. Once again I quote the Apostle Paul who made this point very clear and concise: *2 Corinthians 5:18-21 (HCSB) Everything is from God, who reconciled us to Himself through Christ and **gave us** the **ministry of reconciliation**: 19 That is, in Christ, God was reconciling the world to Himself, not counting their trespasses against them, and He has **committed** the message of reconciliation **to us**. 20 Therefore, we are **ambassadors for Christ**, certain that God is appealing **through us**. We **plead** on Christ's behalf, "Be reconciled to God." 21 He made the One who did not know sin to be sin for us, so that we might become the righteousness of God in Him.* Wow!

In my first book *"Work's Revisited",* I have a chapter entitled *"The Hall of Faith".* That chapter is all about how God not only uses people, but flawed people. People like you and me! Think about this.......just look at who's in this hall of faith. It's filled with people that are flawed is it not? Consider Abraham, a man who lied about his wife calling her his sister because he feared for his life. Something that you and I are certainly capable of and might have done under similar circumstances.

Let's talk about Matthew for a moment here as he is one of the most beautiful stories of Scripture, because it is a story of redemption. Matthew, also known as Levi, was a tax collector. In those days, tax collectors were essentially considered the scum of the earth, because it was rumored that they often cheated other people out of money by overcharging on taxes and pocketing some of that money for themselves. So when Jesus approached Matthew at his tax collector's booth, people probably stared at him, wondering what a righteous rabbi like Jesus was doing associating with this tax collector. Yet he chose to call this man to be one of his disciples, and to follow him and learn his ministry, essentially. Matthew got up, left all of his tax-collecting work behind, and followed Jesus without ever looking back. This disciple ended up writing one of the four Gospels of Scripture, and he has quite the tale to tell.

Finally, one of the most unlikely people that God used to bring about his will was Saul of Tarsus, who later became known as the apostle Paul. Saul was originally a Pharisee, a very prominent religious leader among the Jewish community. He would often harm or kill anyone who claimed to be a Christian, but one day, when he set out on the road to Damascus, he had a vision of Jesus, who explained that Saul's actions were wrong. As a result, he turned his life around, dedicated everything he had to serving Christ, and ended up writing many books of the New Testament. His is a story of how God can take someone who seems to be rebelling against him, turn them around, and cause them to start living for him. Therefore, Paul's story is also a story of redemption and transformation, and proof that if God can use people like him to accomplish his will, then he can use anyone, no matter what their past, present, or future actions have been or will ever be.

In fact I came across these short reminders recently, let this sink in:

~ Noah was a drunk

~ Abraham was too old

~ Isaac was a daydreamer

~ Jacob was a liar

~ Leah was ugly

~ Joseph was abused

~ Gideon was afraid

~ Samson had long hair and was a womanizer

~ Jeremiah and Timothy were too young

~ David was an adulterer and a murderer

~ Elijah was suicidal

~ Jonah ran from God

~ Naomi was a widow

~ Job went bankrupt

~ Peter denied Christ

By now I'm pretty sure you get the picture..........

In response to these marching orders, the real question at hand is this: *"what will you & I do, in fact may I ask this.... what have we done thus far with these orders?"* I once heard a friends of mine many years ago say this: *"revival starts in the heart of just one!"* I couldn't agree with her more! One person can really make a difference. That truly comes into proper perspective when I think that just eleven persons carried the Gospel around the world and that you and I and millions all over are recipients of their efforts even to this day. And believe me when I say that I could easily include many more examples of flawed and broken people that God used all throughout the Bible, both Old and New Testament, but suffice it say we've seen a few very real examples here.

In the next chapter let's talk more in a specific way about whom God uses, you may be surprised with what you hear as you were hopefully surprised with whom you read about in this chapter that God used despite their shortcomings and so we are in good company according to Romans 3:23: (HCSB) *For all have sinned and fall short of the glory of God.*

Chapter 3

Who Is Called To Share?

Over the years I can't recall how many times I have heard this most deadly statement coming out of the mouths of believers from all walks of life: *"Pastor Al, you don't understand, God can't use me"* and then they would go on with their list of reasons why God couldn't possibly use them. And please trust me when I say that I've heard it all, because I really have! I know just about every excuse in the book. So let's deal with just the facts here concerning who is called to share this glorious Gospel.

MOSES – 1st case in point

I'd like to start with Moses, the great and mighty man that God used in a miraculous way to free the people of Israel before Pharaoh who eventually let the people go. But did you know that

Moses didn't start off that way? In fact, when God called Moses to this great and mighty task, the truth be told, Moses sounded like the last guy God should have picked! Just listen to this dialogue as we pick up the story in Exodus 3:9-11 (HCSB) *The Israelites' cry for help has come to Me, and I have also seen the way the Egyptians are oppressing them. 10 Therefore, go. I am sending you to Pharaoh so that you may lead My people, the Israelites, out of Egypt." 11 But Moses asked God, "Who am I that I should go to Pharaoh and that I should bring the Israelites out of Egypt?"* Let's move ahead to Exodus 4:1-17 (HCSB) *Then Moses answered, "What if they won't believe me and will not obey me but say, 'The LORD did not appear to you'?" 2 The LORD asked him, "What is that in your hand?" "A staff," he replied. 3 Then He said, "Throw it on the ground." He threw it on the ground, and it became a snake. Moses ran from it, 4 but the LORD told him, "Stretch out* your hand and grab it by the tail." So he stretched out his hand and caught it, and it became a staff in his hand. 5 "This will take place," He continued, "so they will believe that Yahweh, the God of their fathers, the God of Abraham, the God of Isaac, and the God of Jacob, has appeared to you." 6 In addition the LORD said to him, "Put your hand inside your cloak." So he put his hand inside his cloak, and when he took it out, his hand was diseased, white as snow. 7 Then He said, "Put your hand back inside your cloak." He put his hand back inside his cloak, and when he took it out, it had again become like the rest of his skin. 8 "If they will not believe you and will not respond to the evidence of the first sign, they may believe the evidence of the second sign. 9 And if they don't believe even these two signs or listen to what you say, take some water from the Nile and pour it on the dry ground. The water you take from the Nile will become blood on the *ground." 10 But Moses replied to the LORD, "Please, Lord, I have never been eloquent—either in the past or recently or since You have been speaking to Your servant—because I am slow and hesitant in speech." 11 Yahweh said to him, "Who made the human mouth? Who makes him mute or deaf, seeing or blind? Is it not I, Yahweh? 12 Now go! I will help you speak and I will teach you what to say." 13 Moses said, "Please, Lord, send someone else." 14 Then the LORD's anger burned against Moses, and He said, "Isn't Aaron the Levite your brother? I know that he can speak well. And also, he is on his way now to meet you. He will rejoice when he sees you. 15 You will speak with him and tell him what to say. I will help both you and him to speak and will teach you both what to do. 16 He will speak to the people for you. He will be your spokesman, and you will serve as God to him. 17 And take this staff in your hand that you will perform the signs with."*

Looking at all these verses do you see a man of boldness and confidence? Not by any means, in fact we see the opposite! Moses actually said to God in verse 13 **"Please, Lord send someone else".** Sound familiar?

Let's face it, none of us wants to be put in a tight situation or feel squeezed or forced into sharing Christ with others and the truth we shouldn't don't have to be forced or pushed. Yes, there will most certainly be times where we are going to have our backs up against the wall; I'll call these *"Moses moments".* But if you know the rest of the story, you know that God delivered the nation of Israel and His servant in doing so was no other than Moses, the man who said *"Lord get someone else!"* That should give everyday folks like you and I a lot of hope and confidence.

Ananias – 2nd case in point

I have a message that I share every now and then entitled *"Our Ananias Moment"* Seems to me that anyone who walks with the Lord and desires to be used by Him and who lives faithfully is going to be called upon at some point in their lives to do something extra ordinary for God. There is a great quote out there that says this *"Every day, ordinary people do extra ordinary things"*, boy do I believe that and mainly because I have witnessed it many times over! And Ananias is no exception. We know very little about him in Scripture. What we do know is that he was a Disciple of Jesus from Damascus, so that tells us that at the very least he was a faithful man. And with so little said about him, I don't think it's unreasonable to assume that he was probably just your *"run of the mill"* type of guy, nothing special per see about him. So in this second example we certainly learn this: God uses all kinds of people and simple every day ordinary people are among those whom God desires to use as we'll see here with our friend Ananias. And I love the dialogue when the Lord calls upon him to lay hands on Saul, let's join the text in v. 11 of Act's chapter 9 and see if you can see a similarity between Ananias and Moses. Acts 9:11-16 (HCSB) *11 "Get up and go to the street called Straight," the Lord said to him, "to the house of Judas, and ask for a man from Tarsus named Saul, since he is praying there. 12 In a vision he has seen a man named Ananias coming in and placing his hands on him so he can regain his sight." 13 "Lord," Ananias answered, "I have heard from many people about this man, how much harm he has done to Your saints in Jerusalem. 14 And he has authority here from the chief priests to arrest all who call on Your name." 15 But the Lord said to him, "Go! For this man is My chosen instrument to take My name to Gentiles, kings, and the Israelites. 16 I will show him how much he must suffer for My name!"* Now verse 13 shows us that Ananias like Moses thought that maybe God had the wrong guy he was telling him to go see so he wants to make sure that God isn't making a mistake here, basically saying in a roundabout way: *"Lord are you sure you got the right guy you want me to visit?"* Ananias reminds God who Saul is and God reassures him that it is indeed Saul He wants him to go to. So be ready when your *"Ananias moment"* comes as the good news is that the verses that followed show us that Ananias did indeed do all that the Lord asked him to do and was bold in doing it just like Moses when he was before Pharaoh.

3rd case in point – Members of the Hall of Faith

The truth is I hardly know where to begin here. We have so many examples of flawed and frayed people who can be found in this *"Hall of Faith"* that these examples alone should be enough evidence for you and I that God can and will use anyone who is open to His leading, plus consider that since He is God, frankly He can do what He wants, with whomever He wants, wherever he wants, Amen! Sarah, the women who questioned whether God could give her a child in her age is listed here, Rahab, the prostitute, imagine that a lady of the night if you will is in the Hall of Faith! Samson a womanizer is also mentioned there. So I think we've clearly established who is called to share. God used all kinds of people in the Bible from all kinds of backgrounds and if you have a heart to be used by Him in sharing His word with others, then have **NO** doubt that He can and wants to use **YOU!**

I love this passage from 2nd Chronicles 16:9a: (HCSB) *For the eyes of Yahweh roam throughout the earth to show*

Himself strong for those whose hearts are completely His. Friends if your heart belongs to the Lord, then count on it that at some point He is going to call on you to do something for Him to further His Kingdom in some fashion.

In fact, Pastor Steven J. Cole who writes on Bible.org has an excellent article that I'd like to use an excerpt from that really applies here.

He writes concerning whom God uses: *"Have you ever marveled at how the Lord launched the worldwide movement called "the church"? If He had only asked me, I would have advised Him to do things differently! I would have asked, "What were You thinking when You came up with these men to launch this movement?" I would have said, "In the first place, if You want to launch a movement that is going to impact the world for centuries to come, You need to pick men with the proper education and experience. They should be graduates of* the most prestigious theological institutions in the world. They need to have a track record of impressive results in the ministry. After all, their past performance indicates their future potential. But these guys have no degrees and no achievements!" "Furthermore, You need men of influence who have connections with important wealthy, powerful people. They need to know how to network with the movers and shakers. No offense, but these men have accents that make them sound like hicks from the sticks. They're Galileans! The religious elite in Jerusalem are going to laugh them out of town if they try to persuade them that You are the Messiah."

"Also, You need to pick some men who know how to grow a business. They need to know how to recruit and manage a competent team. They need to know how to read a spread sheet. A Galilean fishing business doesn't cut it! At least get someone with an M.B.A. on *the team! Too bad about that guy, Judas! He would have been a real asset to the cause!"* But to launch the church the Lord chose a bunch of uneducated, unsophisticated Galilean fishermen, who would have been laughed out of the Sanhedrin in Jerusalem. To use Paul's words (2 Cor. 4:7), He picked a bunch of earthen vessels in which to put His treasure, so that the surpassing greatness of the power would be of God and not from any man. The fact that He used such humanly unimpressive men should give us hope that perhaps He can use common people like us to help further His kingdom".

"To reach the world God uses people whom He has given to His Son, who know and obey Him, whom He keeps while they're in this world".

Now add the following passage to the mix: 1 Corinthians 1:26-29 (HCSB) *Brothers, consider your calling: Not* *many are **wise** from a human perspective, not many **powerful**, not many of **noble** birth. 27 Instead, God has chosen **what is foolish** in the world to shame the wise, and God has chosen what is **weak** in the world to shame the strong. 28 God has chosen what is **insignificant and despised** in the world—what is viewed as nothing—to bring to nothing what is viewed as something, 29 so that no one can boast in His presence.*

WOW! Here we are weak, insignificant, despised, and not wise with any nobility. If that isn't enough evidence friends then I'll never convince you that God does indeed do extraordinary things through ordinary people each and every day. It really is time to ask the Lord how He wants to use you and whom He wants you to begin to reach out too. May our Lord help you to begin that journey in Him today.

Chapter 4

Bridges Take Time

In this chapter we are going to begin to look at some of the ways that can help us be more effective in our witnessing opportunities. Now one of the first questions I must ask you is really more of a challenge. *"To what degree are you willing to go to reach even one person for Christ?"* I'll give you 3 examples. First is an old friend from back in the 80's who was a neighbor who loved to bowl. Now to me, nothing is more boring than bowling *(sorry to all the bowlers out there, I mean no disrespect)* but it's just that bowling was probably about the last thing on my list of desired activities and still is, in fact I'm not even sure if I have bowled more than once since that day in the late 80's! However, in this situation of trying to reach my neighbor, let's call him *"Bob"*; it became very obvious that if I wanted to reach him, I'd have to go bowling with him. We also shared a love for music so I had been using that as an opportunity to get to know him, plus I was dealing with his wife whom it became clear to me wasn't very keen on *"religion"*, so getting away to spend time with Bob alone was a priority. And to this day I still remember how bad I was, gutter ball after gutter ball, it was downright embarrassing to be honest, but in time I was able to bring him to a place of knowing who the Jesus of the Bible was. What was so heartbreaking was that a short time later he ended up getting sick and died while still in his late 30's leaving behind his wife and children. I am so thankful that I had that time with Bob to share Jesus and God's salvation plan. I believe I will see him again because he opened his heart to Christ. Now when it comes to food, despite being a native New Englander *(I'm from Connecticut)* I am not much of a seafood person, never have been. But upon meeting a really nice younger couple, it became clear that if I wanted to befriend them in any way I would have to engage in one of their favorite activities, dining out for Sushi. Now nothing is more undesirable to me in the food realm than uncooked fish. All I can say is thank God for California rolls! I ended up labeling this time *"Sushi for Jesus!"* Now to the best of my knowledge this couple did not come to faith, but I was able to at least make a good investment of the Gospel in their lives and sadly for various reasons like leaving the business industry I was in along with moving down South have not stayed in touch with them over the years, *(remember God's word tells us that at times we may be sowers and at other times we may be reapers)* but I am thankful for that opportunity to plant a seed. Last was probably one of my wildest ventures and that was into the arena of CB radio. Now you need to understand that back in the late 80's and early 90's there were a lot of CB radio *(10 meter)* users in the greater Waterbury, Ct. area and I felt a *"tug"* on my heart from the Lord to get involved. The neat thing was that I even got a *"handle"* which was an identification name for when you were *"on air"* broadcasting. In fact the same time that I got this handle name an older couple that I knew who were very sweet who loved the Lord were at a tag sale and she noticed a pin that said *"Good News"* on it and felt the Lord was telling her to buy it for me, no big deal right, wrong! That was the exact name I felt to use on the air so you can only imagine the mighty confirmation I felt when just a few days later without knowing anything she presented that pin to me! Well it didn't take long for me to immerse myself into that *"CB"* culture and in no time I was making new friends and having many conversations, especially with this one individual which ultimately lead to my leading him and his wife to the Lord amongst other things I'll just say, but it was really awesome to see the Lord move during my time on the radio and in fact to this day on Facebook I'm still friends with a few of these people I used to talk to and it's not unusual for them to message me asking for prayer, etc. so please let this be an encouragement to anyone out there who feels a call to do something rather *"strange or offbeat",* of course providing it isn't something against the things of God, I say go for it! So overall, I think you get the picture. Here's what I share with my Congregation and I'd like to share it with you all: *"do not dare to share the Gospel with anyone unless you are also willing to invest the proper time".* Okay so now let's talk about Bridges as it relates to sharing Christ with others.

Building bridges takes time and depending upon what type of weight you plan to carry over that bridge, it can take a real long time, even many years! Coming back to Dr. Leighton Ford and his book *"Good News Is for Sharing"*, on page 116 he writes this: *"How do we move from bridge building to bridge crossing? I would suggest that the next step in personal communication is to be an explorer. When an explorer discovers a new island, he circles until he finds the most likely place to land his boat. A bridge builder has to explore until he finds the most likely spot to span the water. As communicators, we have to explore patiently the lives of others until we find the route God has opened that offers access to their minds and hearts"*. I have always had a saying *"the bridge has to carry the weight"*. For instance, have you ever had a deep or serious conversation with someone you thought was ready for what you had to say, but quickly found out they weren't? The problem was that the bridge you had to this person simply couldn't carry the weight of your conversation and that happens usually when we become impatient or when we try to *"cut corners"* so to speak. Another thing Dr. Ford mentions is that *"bridges are for traffic".* He writes *"bridges are not built for looks, but to bear traffic".* I couldn't agree more and as I mentioned, bridges can also take a **LOT** of time to build. Oh how we need patience in witnessing with others for let's face it, we live in a *"I want it yesterday"* culture, but that's not how it goes when we are trying to win another to Christ. Patience my friend will unquestionably be a main ingredient in your efforts to reach others for Christ so buckle in for the long haul!

And as I have been saying, the stronger the bridge, the more *"weight"* you can begin to send across it. *(Requiring more time of course!)* I am reminded as I write of how many times I have gotten correspondence from people years after our encounter, in fact I must confess that most of the time it's been so long that I can hardly remember that specific contact and conversation. In those cases it took years for the seed to finally germinate and sprout to the point the person committed their life to Christ and then went out to find me. *(These were the days before the internet, not an easy task back then!)* I mention this because I want you to take heart and know that God is always moving *"behind the scenes."* Never give up on your efforts to reach others as the Lord can and will use any circumstance that happens to bring those persons to Him and in some cases as I just mentioned it can be years later. So won't you become a bridge builder for Jesus Christ? As I said earlier, be willing to invest whatever time is required, for we can never put a price tag on even one person, Amen!

Chapter 5

The Room Search

I was in sales for many years, over 25 to be exact. For part of those years I was also a bi-vocational Pastor and it didn't take me long to realize there was a definite connection in sales and evangelizing and it was this, in either case you must take the time to get to know whom you are talking to and also have a real and genuine concern for their needs. The latter truth is the hardest, especially when it came to sales, so many people want to simply *"get in and get out".* Well when it comes to reaching people for Christ, I can tell you, you are usually in for some type of long haul plain and simply. So one of the things I learned along the way was something I ended up naming what it really is! *"The room search".* It requires one thing always: Intentionality. You must be very focused and single minded when you're intentional no matter what you're intentional about. I recently heard Tom Brady, QB of the New England Patriots who just won his 6th Super Bowl talk about when the season starts he becomes *"football centric"*. When I played CYO *(Catholic Youth Organization)* basketball back in the mid 70's I was known as the guy on the team who had *"tunnel vision"*, that's what my Coach called it. Whenever I got the ball, I usually made a bee line for the hoop! That's how intentional one has to be to do the room search. Basically whenever I meet someone at their home, I immediately begin looking around for any item of *"common interest"* that I can find. Now the reason should be obvious right? Well it's not that simple because it isn't just about finding something we can both chat about which makes for everyone feeling easier in communicating. It's also that it didn't take long before I began to realize that just about every person has a metaphorical *"wall"* of sorts around them and this became my way of taking that so called wall down. *(Picture if you can a kind of small castle like turret around a person when you meet them for the first time and as you begin to talk and communicate, you can begin to slowly watch the bricks coming down one at a time as the other person realizes you have an interest in them or whatever common interest item you've both discovered and that you truly care about them or the subject resulting in a feeling that's quite comfortable in communicating together quickly. I've see this happen over and over!)* I have talked with thousands of people from all walks of life over the years and know this to be true without question, keeping in mind that there are always exceptions to the rule, but not too many when it comes to communicating properly resulting in offsetting people's defensiveness at the outset of meeting for the first time. In fact today I think this is far truer than it's ever been. I recently heard a comedian do a sketch on people coming to our door. He talked about how when he was a kid, people loved it when company came over, it was a big deal and back in those days you didn't have to call ahead of time, just show up! Then he launched into a hilarious *(albeit sad)* diatribe of how it is today when someone rings our doorbell. People sort of flip, saying things like *"who can that be"* and getting all shaken up. To be honest he had me almost rolling on the floor because he was dead on. Oh how times have changed! So by doing this room search and finding something as an *"icebreaker" (meaning something common for us to chat about to get things rolling along at the outset)* You'll also see some physical signs that the person is beginning to feel more comfortable or is more relaxed, I've even noticed their facial expressions change to a more comfortable manner, And notice things like when people's arms are folded. That is commonly referred to as a *"defensive"* posture. *(Learn to read what is called "body English")* I can't even recall how many times during our conversation I've seen people suddenly let their arms down or move them to a less defensive position. I call myself a sort of *"jack of all things"*. I do my best to keep up on as much as I can whether it be current events, better ways to communicate including noticing people's bodily movements within communication, stocks, world news, weather or whatever because you just never know when you will need to pull that topic out of the bag so to speak and be able to talk about it intelligently. I'm also a big sports fan so whenever I see something like a team logo or hat, etc. I'm easily off to the races. So friends please stay up on things happening around you, that's healthy and important and trust me, it will pay dividends! The lone caution I have is this, and it's a big one, while I mentioned that there are similarities between sales and evangelizing, what is not similar is that evangelizing is **NOT** selling! Please take immediate notice that an insincere heart can and will be exposed quickly! If there's one thing I know about people *"in the world"* is this, they can pick out a phony in no time, and they can tell when you're giving them what we use to call in my former industry a *"dog and pony show"* and shut you down in no time flat.

Those who know me know I have a deep and genuine love for people of ALL ages, from 8 to 88! And I'm happy to tell you I've never abused the room search nor did it merely for a sale or to just hook someone in, God forbid! I do it because it is a way for me to begin to get to know a person and it is a powerful conversation starter! I mentioned Dr. Ford's book earlier, in one chapter he talks about this in a bit of a different way, but really we are saying the same thing. He calls it

"Common Ground Evangelism" and has a few diagrams, but I'll give you the long and short of it here. Whenever we meet an unbeliever, there will always be areas of common interest somewhere between them and you, 90% of the time. It's hardly ever that there isn't something somewhere that there's common interest between the two of you if you probe enough and ask the right questions. So the key is having some real conversations that lead to those areas of common interest, then it's all about taking the time to share those interests together. Hopefully as the Lord leads, your investment in that person will certainly lead at some point to great openings to share the Good News of Jesus Christ. Another thing I noticed is that when I've entered someone's home, the more I noticed things in their proper place or just a real clean environment, this was a sign I was probably dealing with a *"no nonsense"* type of person, or as they

say a *"get in, get out or get out of my way"* type. This usually meant that such a person wasn't much for small talk or for things insignificant in the daily grind of life. It was most often reflective of a more serious or deep thinking type. I often found myself discussing such topics as Science, History, etc. so as I said earlier being a sort of *"jack of all things"* really pays off with these types of folks. Thus one needs to have an ability to quickly and knowledgeably shift gears on a dime when the conversation requires us to do so.

In closing, once again remember that bridges take time, so make sure your heart is always in the right place friends and I have no doubt whatsoever that God will bless you for your sincere and heartfelt efforts as He has mine over all these years.

Chapter 6

Navigating the Minefields

Just about every person you talk to will usually have some sort of what I can only call *"minefield"* that you will have to navigate through. Notice I didn't say around! I wish I could write here that minefields can be back doored, but that has never been my experience in over 30+ years of witnessing. Minefields in people's hearts are like fear in a sense. Here's what I mean. In order for a person to move forward in their life who has had trouble with fear, they must come to a place where they finally realize they must face that particular fear. In other words, there are no short cuts, no end around, etc., no, they must walk and work through their fear to get to safe harbor, I believe that with all my heart because that's truly the only way I have seen people overcome their fears and get healthy and better.

Consider these passages from God's word.

Isaiah 41:10 (HCSB) **Do not fear**, *for I am with you; do not be afraid, for I am your God.* **I will strengthen you**; *I will help you;* **I will hold on to you** *with My righteous right hand.*

Philippians 4:6-7 (HCSB) **Don't worry about anything**, *but in* **everything**, *through prayer and petition with thanksgiving, let your requests be made known to God. 7 And the* **peace of God**, *which surpasses every thought, will* **guard your hearts and minds** *in Christ Jesus.* In verse 6, the Greek word for worry also means anxious. And anyone who has struggled with anxiousness knows it is a first cousin of fear.

Romans 8:15 (HCSB) *For you did not receive a spirit of slavery to fall back into fear, but you received the Spirit of adoption, by whom we cry out, "Abba, Father!"*

1 John 4:18 (HCSB) *There is no fear in love; instead, perfect love drives out fear, because fear involves punishment. So the one who fears has not reached perfection in love.*

Okay, so recognizing these minefields is crucial when communicating the Gospel to someone. So how do we do this, what are a few ways we can be of help to folks who are struggling? The first is:

- **BY LISTENING**

As a Pastor, I must confess I like to talk; learning to listen and listen effectively has truly taken me a lifetime. But I am thankful that some time ago I was able to get to a point where my ears were always listening for the *"words from the heart"* by a person. Often times I would end up saying something like *"Jim, what did you mean when you said such and such, etc."* And when they explained it, bingo! I usually ended up finding another landmine! And the landmines that people will have are as vast and different as the night is from the day! Every person is different so listen intently and hear their struggles and their concerns and then begin the process of helping them navigate those concerns. One huge landmine that often comes up is this: *"Pastor Al, I'm just mad at God"......* Those are persons I usually find out who have lost a child or loved one or close friend somewhere along in life and simply can't understand why. It's a legitimate landmine. I often respond to that *with "it's okay to be mad at God, He's got big shoulders and he can take it!"* And within no time we are talking it out, or at least beginning to. Learn to develop a way to help people through their difficulties and try to place yourself as much as you can, in their shoes. This is important because if you do your best to *"wear their shoes",* then you will also know why they feel the way they do, and the result is that you will have a deeper understanding and appreciation for why they feel the way they do regardless of whether or not it's correct or right. In fact I have also found this to be true, part of the way for them to overcome this situation is actually just being able to talk about it, just being able to be open and honest! Sometimes that alone brings them half way home friends, if not more of the way as I've heard countless times after a deep conversation discussing a minefield with someone *"well at the very least I sure do feel a lot better, sort of like my load was lightened a little".*

- **By Being Understanding**

This can be a hard one. Consider today how many times now you will hear in a meeting during prayer time *"I have an unspoken request?"* Friends there's a reason why we are hearing this more than ever. And I think it comes down to two concerns people have in the Church today. 1) They are afraid that they will be judged by their fellow Christians and unbelievers feel this just as much! 2) They've unfortunately had someone go around and talk about their situation so they are afraid to talk openly about anything of substance going on personally. So we need to be very loving, graceful and understanding, yes even if what they say to you is unthinkable, terrible or whatever. And thank them for entrusting you with their heart, while assuring them of strict confidence. I will often text or email a person a day or so later who has shared someone sensitive with me going on in their life, usually texting something along the lines of *"thank you for trusting me, I really appreciate that and I'm praying for you and want to help you in any way I can"*. When a person can trust you, wow that will open up a **HUGE** door! Far too many of us sadly have played or want to play Mr. Holy Spirit and have ended up hammering someone who is down, well that never works and I don't think that's the *"Jesus*

Style" to steal the name of a great book by Gayle Erwin. That's why a few pages back I talked about trying to sincerely walk in their shoes which automatically will result in us having more empathy for that person's plight. Next is to be trustworthy, don't go around telling everyone, this is like basic 101, but you'd be surprised how stuff gets around, especially today with social media, etc.

- **Offer Biblical Advise**

Proverbs 3:5-7a will help us here: *Trust in the LORD with all your heart, and do not rely on your own understanding; 6 think about Him in all your ways, and He will guide you on the right paths. 7 Don't consider yourself to be wise; fear the LORD and turn away from evil.* Notice the language in V.7, *"Don't consider yourself to be wise".* Another excellent passage that speaks of giving people illumination and direction is found in Psalm 119:105: *Your word is a lamp for my feet and a light on my path.* A lamp gives illumination, light and a path speaks of giving us direction. So offer the person who is entrusting you with their heart hope from God's word, give them powerful passages of Scripture that apply to their present struggles. Those passages if you look can always be found because the Bible is truly a *"life manual".* Instruction can be always found to help anyone, anytime in God's word!

Learn what specific landmines are prevalent in a person's heart and begin what may be a very slow, loving and understanding process of navigating through that particular mine. Be willing to talk about it whenever that person brings it into the conversation, but I would not recommend however, trying to *"push or force"* that person to talk about it, learn to know when they are ready and what the signs are like them bringing it up in your conversations, etc. regardless of how much it may be keeping them back, they must come to a place themselves hopefully with the Spirit of God's help to be able to open up about it and if you are in the for long haul which is usually the case then the time factor is not of importance right?

- **Help Them Through**

This is what I was talking about at the beginning of this chapter. Help the individual navigate through their problem or situation, walk with them, stand in the gap as the Scripture states. This is ever so important. People who are struggling no matter what the situation often feel defeated because they feel alone! They've lost hope in their isolation and it is our job to walk them through. *(Satan is a master at isolation; know that friends, a person is FAR easier to pick off once they are out on their own away from their support and especially the Lord)* For example, as a pastor I say to my folks often that I will not ask them to do something I haven't already done or something that I'm not willing to do myself lest I be a Pastor who merely *"points"* the way instead of leading the way. By walking them through, you and I will at the same time help them along to that place of safe harbor. We can also call this *"holding their arms up"* for in Scripture in Exodus 17:12 even our brother Moses needed help, so Aaron and Hur got on each side and held his arms up when he grew tired, so we must do likewise for those who have also grown tired struggling their way through their minefield so that we can navigate them safely to the other side. *(What I call safe harbor)* Keep compassion and empathy close to your heart when you are involved in this type of ministry, they will serve you well as they have me.

Chapter 7

Going the Extra Mile

Don't hold this against me, but I have been a diehard Dallas Cowboys fan since 1970. At some point during 1969, the 1st season I remember watching football, I fell in love with the Minnesota Vikings. That was their 1st Super Bowl team known as *"40 for 60"*, meaning 40 players giving it all they've got for 60 minutes out on the field. And I especially liked #11, QB Joe Kapp, what a winner he was, a real leader and a guy who could take a hit and keep fighting, he reminds me of the energizer bunny and for those of you from the 60's, you'll remember John Cameron Swayze who did the Timex watch commercials. Joe Kapp was like that Timex watch, *"he takes a licking and keeps on ticking!"* anyhow, sometime during the 69' season I saw that beautiful helmet with a shining star on it and add to the fact that my Vikings fell hard to the Kansas City Chiefs in Super Bowl IV, 23-7 both put an end to the Vikings being my favorite team, they're my 2nd favorite team now. Well I say all that to say this, my all-time favorite football player, Dallas QB Roger Staubach was once quoted as saying: *"the road on the extra mile has no log jams"*. Well if this is true, and I think it may very well be friends. The problem should be clear and obvious, not too many people are willing to go that extra mile, **BOTH** in and out of the Church in this day, how about you? Back in Connecticut in 1983 there was a lot of excitement because the BGEA *(Billy Graham Evangelistic Association)* announced a series of meetings throughout New England. Dr. Graham would speak at Boston University's Nickerson Stadium, Harvard, Yale and the then Hartford Civic Center in Connecticut's capital City along with his brother in law, Dr. Leighton Ford. *(Whom I've referred to a few times in* *this book)* Now ahead of his crusade team were a series of meeting called the *"Christian Life and Witness Course"* And I can say unequivocally that to this day, this was by far the most effective class or course I have ever attended concerning a most important subject that is woefully neglected in the Body of Christ.......**FOLLOW UP**. It was here that I learned the value of going the extra mile, going *"above and beyond"* to ensure that a person understands what they are doing when they make a commitment to Jesus Christ, along with what it takes to help them in their crucial early months of coming to known our Savior in a personal way. And for the record so many of us forget that it is a commitment, not merely an invitation or one time off thing! This is a major problem in the Body of Christ to this day. All too often we hand a new convert who has just received Christ a nice new Bible, encourage them to read it and basically say *"blessings to you,* *good luck on your new spiritual journey!"* In the words of the former late great sports broadcaster, Dick Enberg: *"Oh My!"*.......

Friends that is **NOT** going the extra mile! Sitting here today writing I'm immediately reminded of two men who played a great part in my early development as a very young Christian, Ivan Nelson and Bob Cronk Sr. Truth is, I'm not sure where I'd be without their invaluable input into my life in those early days. Ivan loved on me, invited me over to his home, made me feel like *"somebody"* and understand that I was this kid off the streets of the Brooklyn section of Waterbury, Ct., where we were all a little crazy growing up there and most certainly raised our fair share of hell in those days, the early to mid-70's. Bob meanwhile would often speak things of great value that I ended up calling *"Bobism's."* He was a man of such wisdom and like Ivan, would also have me up his home and loved on me as well. Both of these men were willing to make an investment in my life which I am so humbled to say *(tears are in my eyes)* that I have been able to go on to do with hundreds, maybe even thousands over the last 38+ years, and all because God used these two men willing to go the extra mile and love on me in those most important early developmental days of walking with my Lord Jesus Christ. Both of those men have long been home with our Lord and most certainly have received a King's reward! From the bottom of my heart, thank you Ivan and Bob for your investment, enjoy the dividends to your accounts in heaven! **Thank you for traveling the road of the extra mile.** So I would definitely say that part of going the extra mile is to be willing to be a mentor to a new or young Christian. Come alongside them, love them just as they are, and help them make needed life changes, mentor them in God's Holy word, have them over your home for dinner and spend some quality time with them. Perhaps the biggest blessing to my wife and I during our time here in Lynchburg, Va. has been the wonderful investment we have been able to make in the lives of our students who attend Liberty University and I'm proud to say Lynchburg College *(now University!)* and CVCC *(Central Virginia Community College)* We've been here 10 and half years as of this writing *(2019)* and we've been able to play a real part in many of their lives, just sitting here I'm thinking of many who have been in our lives as well as some who still are like Breanna, Erica, Meredith, Melissa, Jeremiah, Lacey, Jenny, Hilary, Lisa, Roshel, *(my surrogate daughter)* Abby, Evan, Michael, David, Tyler, Nikki, Chan, Julia, Esther, John, Brianna, Emma, Isaac, Matt, Elsa and trust me I could go on!

Okay, so what does going the extra mile look like? I've listed some things that we'll call:

"Extra Mile Markers"

- **Commit immediately to begin some sort of weekly Bible study together.**

  I highly recommend the Gospel of John as it is the big picture Gospel. Go verse by verse slowly through this book, be in no rush and allow whatever time is needed. Ask them to bring questions from their reading for each session, so you can help them in their understanding. Also encourage them to bring any spiritual questions in general that they may have. You may find that they have had a few misconceptions for years that you can clear up

- **Make it a point to engage in some common ground activity**

Perhaps go to a sporting event of his or her liking as I talked about earlier. The point is to do something they like, yes even if it is bowling, lol! *(Don't just meet to discuss or study spiritual things, make an honest effort to get to know the person and his or her family, just as my friends Ivan and Bob did, you never know, but you may very well end up with a few new friends as well!)*

- **Moderate don't dominate.**

What I mean by that is constantly ask questions, questions like, *"what does that passage mean to you, etc."* As we talked about earlier, be a good listener and be willing to allow at times for the *"train to go off the tracks"*, albeit not too far!"

- **Help them assimilate.**

This is so important! Now I am assuming that the person you have led to the Lord or are meeting with will be open to attending your Church, if not let me say this: *"please don't be shy about inviting them!"* So assuming they are open, help them assimilate, introduce them to your friends. I can't tell you how many times I have witnessed a connection somewhere between your new friend and the person you introduce them to, God is really good at that! So assimilation is critical, especially in those early days. A wonderful passage and promise from God that relates comes from Romans 10:17 (HCSB) *"So faith comes from what is heard, and what is heard comes through the message about Christ".* Being in a Church environment where God's trusted and true word is preached is a GREAT place for your friend to be always! Fellowship and friendship go hand in hand! It really is so cool to watch what God does behind the scenes and sometimes right in front of you which is why after 38 years of serving

Jesus, I am still just as excited about follow up as I was then, just ask anyone who attends Greater Grace Chapel!

- **Teach them to pray**

Helping a person begin **THEIR OWN** relationship with Christ is crucial and will determine whether or not they will continue to stand long after you are gone. Jesus gave us a great model prayer example in Matthew chapter 6 we can follow. Each of us is accountable to God as individuals, thus it is essential that a person stand on their own spiritual two feet. Another excellent spiritually enriching program is what I refer to as *"the Proverb of the day"*. Just as there are usually 30-31 days in a month, so are there 31 Proverbs. Have them commit to reading a proverb each day. Proverb's contains a ton of wisdom and good instruction for everyday life.

- **Get Another Involved**

Get another solid believer who loves people and discipleship *(follow up)* to help you come alongside your new friend. This way you're distributing the load a bit and you can work in tandem in helping your new friend get closer to Christ. That old saying really applies here that *"two are better than one"* so take advantage of that and don't feel like you have to be in control which can lead to actually the person feeling a bit *"handled"* by you. In conclusion, it's important to know who those people are in your local Church who have a heart for just loving on people and helping them grow, be sure to know who they are.

Chapter 8

Scripture Memorization

How is scripture memorization linked to evangelism? Why is it important? Can God supernaturally bless our memory and bring back to remembrance important Scripture verses? I'm reminded of this powerful passage found in John 14:26 (HCSB) *"But the Counselor, the Holy Spirit—the Father will send Him in My name—will teach you all things and remind you of everything I have told you".*

There are a few very good reasons why memorizing scripture is important to soul winning. Let's investigate.

One example is built around the truth of John 14:23-26. The revelation here is that the Holy Spirit will bring to remembrance all that Jesus has stated to us! *(Also see Luke 24:1-8)* And keep in mind that there's also a flip side and that is: If you've never taken the time to read what Jesus said, that lack of study and commitment won't pay off when we're in a situation that requires memorization of God's word. *(Now of course the Spirit can certainly supernaturally bring passages out of nowhere, but God always blesses faithfulness!)* Plus we are commanded to do the following in 2 Timothy 2:15: *Be diligent to present yourself approved to God, a worker who doesn't need to be ashamed, correctly teaching the word of truth.* Being a *"worker"* or as many translations put it *"workman"* means also to be a teacher and like any good teacher, hours of faithful study **MUST** be put in. It would not be good for us using any of those 25 verses out of context would it?

Another is that we as believers recognize that there are certain areas of God's word that are anointed and appointed to a particular area of life. For instance: Ephesians 5:22-29 gives us great instruction for the family. John 17 *(all)* which is really the Lord's Prayer is a prayer for unity among all believers, and Romans 8:1-8 shows us there is true freedom from condemnation when we live according to God's word and walk in His ways. If we agree and see that God's word is indeed as Paul said in 2nd Timothy 3:16-17, *"Profitable for teaching and reproof"* so that the person who wants to be used of God can be equipped for every good work, then we can move into the area of the memorization of specific scriptures that God has provided in His word for us in Evangelism. Some of these passages are really good for one on one, others for when you have maybe three or four persons around.

Next, I will list those 25 passages that I have found that I continually use as they have repeatedly come up over and over again in my efforts of reaching others for Christ over 38+ years. Please make a real commitment to learn them until you are fully able to commit them to memory and can quote them verbatim. Also, be sure you use them within their proper context lest we handle God's word carelessly as we've already mentioned. And don't forget the benefits of the person who meditates on God's Word in Psalm I and the one who delights to do God's will in Psalm 40:1-3, 8. Next I will share each verse and a short interpretation on its use specifically in outreach from my many years of experience out in the field.

Our List of 25

- **Romans 5:8-9**
  (I remember once quoting this verse to a man who loved to fish, when I seemed stuck a bit, I asked him this question "do you clean the fish before you catch them?" suddenly he fully understood what this passage was saying that yes, even in his sinful

present state (he was being very honest with me) Christ came right in the middle of exactly where he is to offer Him forgiveness and life eternal)

- **Romans 10:9-10**
  (These two verses offer us a very clear picture of the path to salvation, it requires belief and confession. These two verses also work well with an in depth explanation of John 3:3)

- **Romans 3:23**
  (All means exactly what it says, ALL, no one is righteous in God's eyes!)

- **Matt 6:33**
  (If people could just get a hold of this verse, oh my how their lives would change! Jesus made a very direct promise, place Him and the things of God first in your life and all that you need finances, a home, relationships, everything will fall into place!)

- **Romans 6:23**
  (God really is the perfect balance, the scales are level, the gift of God is eternal life through Christ on one side and on the other are the wages of sin which is death)

- **John 3:3**
  (Always frame this in its proper context. See chapter 9 for more on this passage)

- **John 3:16-17**
  (Never quote 3:16 without verse 17, they go together!)

- **John 1:11-12**
  (Because salvation is a gift, we must receive it! I can bring you a gift, but it's not yours until you take it)

- **John 10:10**
  (I always let people know that there are two plans for your life, God's plan for an abundant life or Satan's plan to

destroy, steal and kill so make sure you chose the right plan friends!)

- **John 14:6**
  (This is the verse that will most often get you into a bit of trouble. I will never forget the response I got once when I shared this verse a few years back with someone. "If you believe that you're so narrow minded you could look through a key hole with both eyes!" But the truth be told, this is usually where your conversation will get more serious as people in today's pluralistic culture scoff at the idea of a singular truth or of anything exclusive so beware friends. I've heard it said that sharing Jesus as the only way to God in this Society of ours is akin to waving a red cape in front of a bull!)

- **John 14:27**
  (A great passage for those you talk to who suffer with anxiety or

depression. I would also include 1st Peter 5:7 as well)

- **1st John 5:13**
  (Oh how people need assurance and this passage speaks of exactly that)

- **Psalm 1:1-3**
  (Great verses on the blessings bestowed by God upon those who are willing to seek after Him in contrast to the wicked as the remaining verses detail)

- **Proverbs 14:12**
  (Choose the right road; travel the correct path, for the road to death seems right the Scripture says!)

- **Revelation 3:20**
  (It's interesting that in the proper context Jesus is standing at the door of the Church because he's outside! However, He does also stand at the door of our hearts as He is a

gentleman and will not knock it down as God has granted humans with a freed will)

- **James 2:17-19**
  (What a great passage on belief! And notice that even Demons believe and they even tremble!)

- **Genesis 6:3**
  (Oh the pain we cause God and others when we go astray, running from God almost always ends in heartbreak)

- **Hebrews 9:27**
  (This is a particularly good passage for use with our Catholic friends who say that there's a place (Purgatory) where one can somehow gain a 2nd chance at salvation)

- **2nd Corinthians 6:2**
  (Today is always the day of salvation, never put off to tomorrow what can

be done today as there may not be a tomorrow as James mentions!)

- **2nd Corinthians 5:21**
  (Simply put, this passage tells us that Christ did for us what we could never do for ourselves)

- **Isaiah 1:18**
  (God is a reasoning God, I sure am glad about that, aren't you?)

- **Daniel 12:2**
  (The idea of eternity is nothing new as this is an Old Testament passage, thus the question, where will we spend eternity?)

- **Ephesians 2:8-9**
  (In the provision of salvation, there is absolutely nothing you or I can ever do to earn salvation, this passage makes that crystal clear)

- ***Titus 3:5-6***
  (Like Ephesians 2:8-9 this passage also makes it clear that we can do nothing on our own to earn salvation in anyway)

- ***Psalm 66:16***
  (Here's an excellent passage where we are told to speak of what God has done for us!)

Go on to study and learn these verses *"inside out"* by finding all the background on them you can. As I mentioned earlier, study them slowly, learn to build analogies around them, learn to use everyday circumstances with them. Start with the first one and do not move on to the next one until you have the verse down completely by memory. I use this three times principle when it comes to names. I will repeat a person's name three times in a row slowly and lo and behold I've always ended up pretty much remembering that person's name. Try that here, only repeat the verse more like ten times in a row and start to speak it out without looking it up and you will find yourself remembering more each time you do and stay on that verse for a few days before moving on once you have it down. I know and believe that as you put these verses into practice and ask God for both a blessed memory and boldness like Peter at Pentecost, you will begin to see people respond to your efforts as God's Word never returns unto him void! *(Empty)* and you can **NEVER** make a mistake by sharing His Holy Word, no matter what the other person's response and frankly if they respond in an ugly or mean fashion, that can actually be a good thing as I've mentioned elsewhere. Such a respond means that you've obviously hit a nerve of sorts so keep digging! *(Isaiah 55:11)*

Chapter 9

What Did You Say and What Does That Mean?

I have no doubt that many of you who have been in *"Church world"* for a while have heard of the language *"Christianese."* Friends, I am here to say that it does exist whether you have heard of it or not! And it's been around for a very long time. It didn't take me long after I came to know Christ back in the late Autumn of 1980 that there was a similar *"language"* that these Christians used and it contained some words that were pretty unfamiliar and funny sounding to me at the time. I heard people say they were *"saved"*; they spoke of *"rapture"*. Some even declared boldly that they were *"washed in the blood!"* Man, I thought to myself, I have to learn this *"coded"* language. And then of course there was this translation of the Bible many of them clung to called *"The King James Version"* that had words like *"saith"* and *"believeth"* and others like *"thou"* and *"thee."* Now the last thing I want to do is insult any of my friends or readers who still use the KJV, but my biggest reason for not using it today, other than its documented inaccuracies, *(a discussion for another time and place!)* is because we no longer speak *"Elizabethan"* English, the basic language of the KJV. *(King James Version)* For instance, when I see a friend I don't say *"how art thou?"* so why would I want to use a translation that makes it even more difficult to understand the Bible when it is already hard enough in 2019? And if you want a brief solid Biblically historic reason consider that back in the day when the New Testament was being written in the Greek language, two types of Greek prevailed, the Classical and the Koine. Only the educated spoke the Classical Greek, but pretty much everyone spoke the Koine, thus it is no coincidence that the New Testament was translated in Koine. The point is this, God wanted **EVERYONE** to have access to His Holy word and to be able to understand it, make sense?

So with this important backdrop, I want to present to you the seven words in *"Christianese"* you and I should never use, **WITHOUT** explaining them properly. In other words, I don't think in today's society these are *"stand alone"* words, with the meaning of words changing all the time, consider a word like tolerance, what it meant 30 years ago it does not mean today! *(Due to the meaning of words changing over time is part of my concern for not using the KJV)* These words need explaining as the average Joe or Mary who doesn't know Christ personally probably has little to no idea what they mean, or worse yet, they have a very distorted understanding of these biblically important words. Before I share them let's talk about why that is the case.

Satan, who has had a 6,000 year head start and who is the master of deception has dived head first into our vernacular, he's been manipulating and changing words for year's friends! And hasn't he done the same thing to God's word and rather effectively I hate to admit? His twisting of God's word is evident in two clear examples, one from the Old Testament and one from the New. Shortly after God created Adam and then Eve, Satan came lurking along in the form of a serpent. Let's pick up the text in Genesis 3:1-5 (HCSB) *Now the serpent was the most cunning of all the wild animals that the LORD God had made. He said to the woman, "Did God really say, You can't eat from any tree in the garden'?" 2 The woman said to the serpent, "We may eat the fruit from the trees in the garden. 3 But about the fruit of the tree in the middle of the garden, God said, 'You must not eat it or touch it, or you will die.'* **4 'No You will not die!'** *the serpent said to the* woman. 5 *"In fact, God knows that when you eat it your eyes will be opened and you will be like God, knowing good and evil."* Notice how he challenges God right off the bat and adds his ever present twist and then goes on to make an appeal to the senses. Basically trying to convince them that God is somehow *"holding back"* from them! Rather crafty and cunning indeed. Then in Matthew 4, Satan came to Jesus Himself and tried putting his twist again on the Holy Scriptures, we pick up in Matthew 4:5-7 (HCSB) *Then the Devil took Him to the holy city, had Him stand on the pinnacle of the temple, 6 and said to Him, "If You are the Son of God, throw Yourself down. For it is written: He will give His angels orders concerning you, and they will support you with their hands so that you will not strike your foot against a stone." 7 Jesus told him, "It is also written: Do not test the Lord your God."* Once again Satan tries to twist God's word, but like Jesus, may our response be God's word in its proper context, amen!

Okay, the following words are words I believe we should never use without giving the proper background and we must always frame them in their proper context. Here is my list of 7:

The 7 Words You Should Never Use Without Proper Explanation/Framing

- **Saved** I learned this one the hard way. Once I was talking to someone about Jesus early in my Christian walk and asked them *"are you saved?"* the guy looked at me quite puzzled and responded with: *"sorry, but I didn't know I was lost!"* Needless to say, that was the last time I ever said that without putting it in proper perspective.

- **Born Again**   This term has been turned on its head over the last 30 years more than the 1st Amendment! **NEVER**, ever use this term without a definite framing of its proper meaning. This is the most misused of all the words on my list by far. I'll never forget an experience I had with a young lady probably in the 80's. When I told her I was born again, I'm not sure if it was a vision or just a *"moving picture"* above her head God was giving me, but her facial expression changed dramatically as I saw this picture above her head. It was as though I could see people yelling, screaming and falling all over the floor; it was then and there I vowed to always explain this term. Satan has jumped right in the middle of those two words to confuse people in a big way. Back in the 80's there was a very popular love song which had the tag line *"when I'm with you I'm born again."* Then Jeep Eagle came out with a series of ads that boldly claimed their vehicle was *"born again for the road!"* In short, today so many people have **NO** idea what this really means so just in case there is any confusion, I'll explain in detail in the next chapter what this term actually means Biblically and how we should explain it in *"layman's"* terms.

- **Repent**   I may get some folks upset by including this word because after all what were the first words Jesus spoke in Mark's Gospel account? Was it not Mark 1:15 (HCSB) *"The time is fulfilled, and the kingdom of God has come near. Repent and believe in the good news!"* But as important as this word is, and it is important, it is also badly misunderstood in today's world. It sounds *"religious, christianese"* and so it must be explained friends.

- **Washed in the Blood** If there was ever an *"insider's"* phrase in Christianity I would imagine that this is it! I just can't even see **WHY** anyone would want to use this term when talking to a non-believer? My suggestion is to stay away from this term when speaking to those who do not know Jesus Christ.

- **Rapture** While millions have certainly heard of the rapture, again it is vastly misunderstood. And add to that the fact it is a sort of scary word to those who do not know Christ. It brings up thoughts of the end of all time, not that that is in and of itself a bad thing, but far too many people have come to Christ by the *"turn or burn"* method and already feel that Christians can be "heavy handed". It should be clear by now many generations later that we didn't have a lot of success as far as *"staying power"* with people using that method and needless to say I don't think we will by using this word. This is a word that should be answered slowly and carefully, but **ONLY** after the other person or you brings it up somewhere down the road, but certainly not in or around the beginning of meeting a person and sharing Christ with them, at least that's what I think.

- **Holy Ghost**   Again, a bit scary to folks, I remember when I first heard this in the KJV of the Bible and was always a little uncomfortable thinking of God's Spirit as a *"ghost"* or apparition, etc. Just stick with the more proper Biblical term Holy Spirit, you will be helping the other person and will be a much more effective communicator of God's word.

- **Religion** Here's another word whose meaning has morphed into something other than what the Bible teaches it to be. Consider James definition here: James 1:26-27 (HCSB)*"If anyone thinks he is religious without controlling his tongue, his religion is useless and he deceives himself. 27 Pure and undefiled religion before God the Father is this: to look after orphans and widows in their distress and to keep oneself unstained from the world"*. In my life group, I recently threw this troubled word in our world today out there and some of the comments were rather revealing. I heard definitions like: *"empty, ridged, cold, generic",* that last one really hit me as being true in our world today. After all Islam or Buddhism are Religions as well. So this is a word that must be framed in a proper context like the other six. There are many *"Religion's"* out there and an interesting point is that practically all of them mention Jesus at some point somewhere in their writings or teachings, but how interesting is it that Jesus **NEVER** mentions **ANY** of them?

In short, what I'm saying is how you communicate the Good News is very important. Speak in a way where the hearer can understand you in a clear and yet concise way. Remember, we live in an *"ADD"* world friends, people can't take in too much these days, in fact I make it a point to not preach beyond 30 minutes on a Sunday morning, unless of course I sense the

Holy Spirit is leading me to speak longer. The main reason I do so is because I am well aware that people's attention spans are far shorter than they once were these days with all the gadgets we have and then add social media to the mix! So knowing this about people today, in another chapter I will stress being able to give your testimony together with sharing the Gospel in or around 5 minutes. Now you may think that five minutes is not a long time, but we'll talk about that later. Below is a diagram of what I call *"God's Plan to Man"* based off the four spiritual laws. I can easily share it about 2/3 minutes.

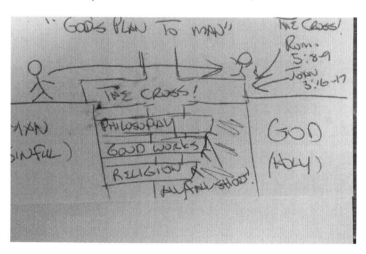

Chapter 10

Born Again?

Ok, this term is important enough that I wanted to tackle it head on in its own chapter. That's how important it is that we communicate exactly what this term means Biblically friends. When I think of born again, I also think of another subject that Christians always seem to have a real hard time explaining and that's the Trinity or Tri-Unity of God. *(God the Father, God the Son and God the Holy Spirit)* These are things we should learn early on, but as I mentioned earlier all too often when a person comes to know the Lord we hand them a nice new fresh Bible and say *"good luck!"* So for the sake of making sure we all understand the correct biblical definition I'd like to use the following article from bibleask.org:

 "Jesus gives the answer to this question, "'I tell you the truth, no one

can see the kingdom of God unless he is born again.' 'How can a man be born when he is old?' Nicodemus asked. 'Surely he cannot enter a second time into his mother's womb to be born!' Jesus answered, 'I tell you the truth, no one can enter the kingdom of God unless he is born of water and the Spirit. Flesh gives birth to flesh, but the Spirit gives birth to spirit. You should not be surprised at my saying, "You must be born again"'" (John 3:3-7). The phrase born again literally means created a new—a spiritual transformation. Being born again, is an act of God whereby eternal life is imparted to the person who believes (2 Corinthians 5:17; 1 Peter 1:3; 1 John 2:29). Paul explains why we need to be born again "For all have sinned and fall short of the glory of God" (Romans 3:23). Sinners are spiritually "dead." But when they receive spiritual life through faith in Christ, they become alive.

Trusting in Jesus Christ as the One who paid the penalty of our sins is the way to be "born again." Paul clarifies, "For it is by grace you have been saved, through faith—and this not from yourselves, it is the gift of God—not by works, so that no one can boast" (Ephesians 2:8-9). After faith, comes the decision to follow Christ in repentance "Therefore, if anyone is in Christ, he is a new creation: the old has gone, the new has come" (2 Corinthians 5:17). Daily connection to the Lord through the study of the Word, prayer and witnessing transforms our lives. "Abide in me, and I in you. As the branch cannot bear fruit of itself, except it abide in the vine; no more can ye, except ye abide in me" (John 15:4). As we yield to the Lord daily, His Spirit does the work of change in us. This is the miracle of transformation. And God gives the promise of salvation to the believer "Yet to all who received him, to those who believed in his name, he gave the right to become children of God" (John 1:12-13).

Let me expound by using the original language the New Testament was written in, Greek. (*Koine Greek which means the everyday Greek that all the people spoke*) Born again in Greek is *"gennao-anothen,"* phonetically pronounced as: ghen-nah-o - an-o-then.

Gennao translated into English means to procreate or regenerate, to be born of. Anothen means: from above, from the first, the very top.

So when we put these two together we have Jesus saying that unless a person is *"born or regenerated from above, (God) the very top, in a spiritual sense He will not see the Kingdom of God".* In other words, we were all born once physically, now we need a spiritual birth, a regeneration if you will spiritually from God to begin to live, walk and serve God and His Kingdom. This spiritual rebirth goes hand in hand with the Apostle Paul stated about confessing, believing and receiving Christ into our lives in Romans 10:9-10 so I will usually go right to that passage after explaining born again as it is a proper extension of that term's meaning.

It's really not complicated when you take it apart for someone and as I've already made clear, far too many people do not know the proper definition of born again. So in your witnessing efforts always be ready to *"shift into low gear"* slow down and explain in detail when it comes to using these two words. I'm certain you will find your efforts to be more effective and successful because as I mentioned earlier, I meet Christians far too many times who have claimed to know the Lord for many years who still can't properly explain the term born again so we can only imagine what those who don't know the Lord think of it and that not ought to be friends.

Chapter 11

Popcorn Testimony

I can hear many of you saying *"what on Earth does a popcorn testimony mean?"* Back in the mid to late 80's I was involved with our local FGBMFI chapter. The Full Gospel Businessmen's Fellowship International. A wonderful organization started by Demos Shakarian. We would hold a dinner every month at a local restaurant, usually at a nice place and it was our job to invite our family and friends to come out for dinner and hear a speaker give his testimony. We were fortunate to have some world renowned speakers during my time there in the mid-80's. Well as a sort of warm up, we'd have what we called a popcorn testimony, this is where a person would get up and have just 5-10 minutes max to give their testimony. And trust me when I say that one of the most *"painful"* things in the meeting would be listening to a guy get up and ramble on for twice that long and those who did usually never saw the platform again! So what I want to talk to you about is learning to give your testimony while at the same time share the Gospel in roughly 5 minutes! Now you may think that's impossible, but try this. Just sit down and look at your watch *(or phone these days)* and just be completely silent for 5 minutes. You will be shocked at how long that actually is! I did TV for 5 years and trust me, just allowing 15-20 seconds of what we called *"dead air"* was excruciating. So how might one give their testimony and share the Gospel within the time allotted? Here are a few points to touch on in the order I present them:

- Start with your religious upbringing or lack thereof....be brief, but don't rush your words. Talk about your own spirituality, basically where you were at spiritually before your conversion.

- Talk about how you were introduced to Christ, was it someone else, was it what you saw in them, etc.?

- Talk about your life since your conversion, what has it been like walking with the Lord, etc.?

- Last, ask the person if they would also like to know Christ in a personal way, let them know that salvation, albeit free for us, cost God everything because He gave up His one and ONLY Son at Calvary!

Now, start to learn to intersperse *(insert)* various passages of Scripture that bolster these points, for instance, here's a few of our 25 verses that I'll use along with a point.

In talking about your own spiritually it could sound something like this. *"Joe, I really thought that I was okay in life, I thought that if I didn't murder anyone or do anyone serious harm, I'd be okay before God, in fact there is a verse in the Bible from Proverbs 14:12 that really spoke to me when I read it, "there is a way (road/path) that seems right to man, but the end thereof is the way of death". It was then I realized I was on that wrong road Joe and that I needed a personal relationship with Christ and since I invited Him into my life I have started to think as He does!* On another point, it could sound this way: *"Mary, since I made a personal commitment to Jesus I can't tell you the peace I feel and then I read where Jesus Himself spoke of this peace in the book of John chapter 14 and verse 27: "Peace I leave with you. My peace I give to you. I do not give to you as the world gives. Your heart must not be troubled or fearful. I can really relate to that, He's made a tremendous difference in my life and I* have a real peace that I've never experienced before!"

And last it can sound something like this: *"Bill, the good news is that you also like me can know this wonderful savior on a personal level, the Bible makes it clear that Jesus died for all, you, me and the entire world. Romans 5:8-9 says this: But God proves His own love for us in that while we were still sinners, Christ died for us! 9 Much more then, since we have now been declared righteous by His blood, we will be saved through Him from wrath". And notice Bill that the Bible doesn't say God thought about it, but rather He demonstrated it, God is a God of demonstration!* So friends learn to strategically place some of the 25 verses I gave you in chapter eight into some of these points. It will make your witnessing efforts that much more effective and precise.

Chapter 12

Dos and Don'ts in the Field

In this chapter, I want to discuss some good ways to share in places like parking lots of Walmart's or supermarkets, street witnessing efforts, basically anywhere out *"in the field"*. So here are some dos and don'ts that I have learned over time.

- **Here's a do:** When at a parking lot of a place like Walmart take some time and look around for people waiting in their cars, this usually results in a chance to have a good conversation with someone as they are not going anywhere! So keep an eye out for folks sitting in their cars as you will definitely have a good opportunity to share and have their full attention.

- **Here's a don't**: Never hand any literature you have to folks going into the establishment as that usually causes the management to get a bit upset as they see folks one after another coming into their store with flyers, etc. Always make sure you hand such information only to people who are on their way back to their cars or as I just shared if they are sitting in their vehicles. The idea is to be as non-evasive as possible.

- **Here's a do:** Always have some good literature to hand out. I usually go with a flyer about our Church along with a few tracts, nothing to heavy, just basic information. I also have my secretary from time to time make up a post card 3 X 5 sort of handout that looks like this on the next page:

- **Here's a don't:** Never be argumentative! Sadly in this day and age some people feel rather strong about the topic of Religion in general. Many are just looking for an argument so it's important to know when it's time to *"cut bait"* so to speak with someone lest it escalates into an argument. Often when I'm going door to door, those coming with me for the first or second time will ask me why I seemed to cut short a conversation and I will explain that it's due to where it was going, a place that usually nothing good can come from. So ask the Lord for godly discernment when you sense a conversation going wrong. In my early days of talking to Jehovah's Witnesses for example I was glad to play what I have come to call *"spiritual ping pong"* by throwing scriptures back at each other, but I no longer spend time doing that for there are far too many people out there who are willing and ready to hear God's word! Here's one of the tracts I've written that I bring with me as an additional handout.

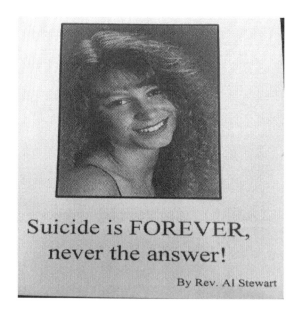

Suicide is FOREVER,
never the answer!

By Rev. Al Stewart

- **Here's a do:** Always bring a little book with you, like that old American Express card commercial, *"never leave home without it!"* Throughout this book I have spoken in earnest about follow up. This book is where you can store all names, emails, cell numbers and addresses so that you can follow up effectively and quickly with each person. This is probably the most important of the dos and don'ts to be honest. If we are not going to get their information and then follow up in a timely manner, what is the point of going out, make sense? So we need to have some good discipline in understanding how important it is to follow up as quickly as possible. Part of my reason for following up quickly is due to what Jesus in the parable of the sower mentioned in Matthew 13. Let's pick up in the text at verse 3: *"Then he told* *them many things in parables, saying: "Consider the sower who went out to sow. 4 As he sowed, some seed fell along the path, and the birds came and devoured them.* **5 Other seed fell on rocky ground where it didn't have much soil, and it grew up quickly since the soil wasn't deep. 6 But when the sun came up, it was scorched, and since it had no root, it withered away.** *7 Other seed fell among thorns, and the thorns came up and choked it. 8 Still other seed fell on good ground and produced fruit: some a hundred, some sixty, and some thirty times what was sown. 9 Let anyone who has ears listen."*

Notice what happened to the seed in verses 5 and 6, the seed grew fast, quickly. I can't tell you how many people will say this to me and I believe at that moment they mean it

"Pastor Al, thank you for coming here, I will absolutely be at service tomorrow, you can count on it!" Just for the record, for every 30 who say that, 1 will actually show up…..how sad it that? See, there's no root in these folks we are talking to, they are just starting and you and I better believe that Satan is going to jump on that person, or one of his cohorts for sure to do all he can to stop them from coming by any means possible. I once had a family who were coming to church for the very first time tell me that as they were walking out the door, a 6 foot mirror they had on the wall feel and crashed into a thousand pieces, thankfully the day before I told them that the enemy was going to do all he could to stop them so they needed to beware. They looked at each other in amazement and said "this is exactly what Pastor Al told us? And thankfully they walked up came to service got a touch from the Lord

again and cleaned up when they got home! Can you see now why time is off the essence; Jesus is telling us that in the parable, two of the other seeds get knocked out the box right away too! So friends please, please, please get back to folks ASAP, it's really crucial as we have seen.

Chapter 13

Going Door To Door

I came to know Christ in a personal way *(Born Again!)* back at the end of August, 1980. The woman who initially shared Jesus with me was also involved in a group known as the *"Dawn Bible Students"* under the influence of Charles Taze Russell, the founder of the Watchtower Bible and Tract Society in Pittsburg, Pa. *(Modern Jehovah's Witnesses)* they were one of many splinter groups that started shortly after the time of Russell's death. The new President, *"Judge"* Joseph F. Rutherford took the organization in a vastly different direction both organizationally as well as doctrinally while amassing complete control over the Watchtower organization which caused these splinter groups to form. I was involved with the Dawn Bible students for only a short period of time thankfully, maybe six months before I realized there was a huge difference between Russell's teaching and the Bible. *(It's interesting to note that Russell taught that a person could only fully understand the Bible by reading along with his six volumes and that if a person was to just read the Bible alone they would "fall into error and darkness", a common theme among pseudo-Christian sects)* I say all that to say this is how I became interested initially in door to door work knowing that Jehovah's Witnesses were very active that way which is another story in and of itself, think about it, how sad is it that you are getting a knock on the door from what seems like everyone except Christians! It's heartbreaking to be honest. So it didn't take long for me to realize and see that Christians needed to be active in this way and sooner before later. Of course as is often the case I'm afraid, many of my Christian friends and even some leaders in the Church I was attending were very negative at the idea of my going door to door. I must say that came as a shock to me and as a young Christian as well it wasn't very encouraging. Now my first Pastor was a great man and he was 100% supportive, but he received some *"flack"* from at least one or two of his Elders. To this day I would have loved to have been a fly on the wall to hear their arguments against me going door to door and witnessing about Jesus to people while giving away Bibles.......*"we can't have a young man going around knocking on people's doors, heaven forbid!"* I simply can't imagine what their concerns were and why they were not congratulating me instead of coming against me, especially when it was hard not to notice that whenever there was a dinner social of any kind the place was packed, but when we had evangelism class, it was my Pastor and I, the new convert. In any case, I quickly realized upon going out why both Kingdom Hall's and Mormon Wards were full on Sundays. It wasn't long before I found that people were then and still are now wide open to discussions, truth is they've always been! And I can honestly say that over the course of my life some of the best people I've met also became some of the strongest Christians I know right up to today via my door to door ministry. Friends, there is a **whole new world** waiting out there for those of you who have a genuine love for people. I started going door to door in 1981 and today in 2019, some 38 years later and maybe 100,000+ doors behind me I am just as excited about going out on Saturday mornings as I was then! I can easily and may very write a book one day just about those experiences I've had over those years.

- **Fruitfulness Issue**

This is usually one of the first objections that come up when you mention door to door ministry. You will undoubtedly hear statements like this: *"the percentage is so low that it's really not worth it or fruitful".* To be honest my initial thought is this: *"can we really put a price tag on even just one soul as I've mentioned earlier?"* Sure it may not be the most successful way from strictly a numbers point of view, but I can tell you that the many I have had come to the Lord has made it more than worth it and what about all those over the years I've spoken with who then moved and later followed up in their search for Christ in their lives and are now a part of a local Church? I could easily devote a chapter to all the people I have heard from that way! In the end analysis I would say that it comes out to somewhere between 2-3% response based on 100,000 people. If I had to guess I think I've prayed with anywhere from 2,000 to 2,500 people and so to me that's a pretty good number. Again, this is really a guess. And as I stated, this is not including all those who followed up later at some point and I am positive based on the calls and letters I've gotten over these last 38+ years that the percentage would be more like 4 or 5% with those included. Then I was recently reminded by my friend, Pastor Steve Willis who said; *"Al, you're talking addition here, now think of it in terms of multiplication!"* *"What about all the people who were reached by the ones you reached?"* I got to thinking he's 100% correct! So the number could easily go as high as 7 or 8%, not a bad return at all friends.

So don't buy into the fruitfulness statement, do what God tells you to do, what you believe you should be doing, for that is what matters as the old Baptist Hymn puts it*: "trust and obey for there is no other way".*

- **Going Equipped**

When I go door to door I have found this time to be the best, Saturday morning starting no earlier than 10:00 am. People are usually up by then and will answer the door. Now of course you're going to wake a few folks up, that's inevitable unfortunately, but they usually understand. Next get yourself a small notebook with about 50/75 pages, like a 3x5 book or even 2x4. Use this book only for your door to door or street witnessing follow up's. When you have a good conversation with someone, always *"strike the iron while it's hot"* so to speak, ask them if they are on Facebook, tell them you want to friend them so you can connect them with your Church's Facebook page, which is an excellent way to connect as they usually check out the page. Then ask them for an email address. At Greater Grace Chapel, *(GGC)* every Wednesday we send out what we call the *"Grace Vine"*, it's our weekly communique to let everyone know what's going on and of course we add these new folks to the weekly list. So it makes this an excellent follow up tool. Last, ask them for a cell number, tell them up front that you want to follow up with them as you are hopefully also inviting them to your Church service. When I ask for their number I usually say something along these lines: *"Now Mr. Jones, what good would it be if I came here today and told you as I have about this wonderful Savior of mine named Jesus, then shook your hand and was gone, is that real effort or showing you God's love?"* Friends I can tell you without question that eight out of every ten folks I talk to give me all three with no problem, email, cell and Facebook info. Remember, if you don't ask you won't get and they probably are not going to offer that information. Be bold! Next make sure you have a proper handout as this is crucial, leave them something tangible. On the next page is a picture of the front and back of our GGC two page *(four sided)* brochure. We hand these out to every door as they are not expensive and are very nice looking in two colors. Simply go down to your local printer in town as it doesn't have to be

anything fancy, just something nice,
clean and with the proper information.

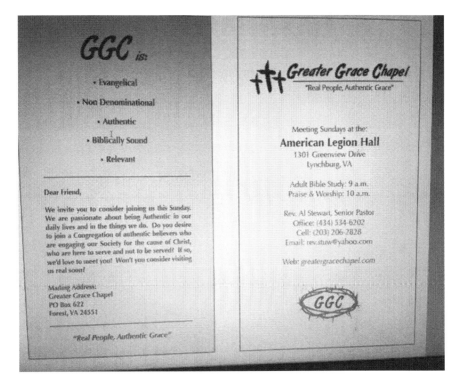

These brochures contain all the
necessary information needed like our
name, place, location and time of Bible
study and service, etc. And the two
inside pages have my picture and a
short bio as Senior Pastor and the other
page has information about our

ministries and what we do. We've had many people visit us simply because we left the flyer folded against their doorknob so I should mention here, make sure every door is left a flyer if they do not answer or are not home. *(There is a difference!)* Sadly in this day and age, many people are frightened to answer their doors if they are alone, or they think you are Jehovah's Witnesses or Mormons *(not Christians how sad!)* so just leave the flyer against their doorknob or between the screen and storm door if they have one. Last year a young man, Alex who moved down from Pittsburg to attend Liberty University got one of the flyers we left at his apartment and started attending GGC and we've become friends as we both share a love for those caught up in Mormonism and this coming August because of him attending his sister and brother in law shortly after they started attending will be taking over our Young Adults ministry and he is now leading our adult bible study, all because a flyer was left on his brother in law's door! In fact, this past Sunday we had a female visitor who came because she said to me that *"someone left a GGC brochure in a flower by her door!"* so you simply never know who will end up visiting friends.

- **Ice Breakers**

We often use these to get a conversation started. When a person answer's the door I usually start with this: *"Hi, my name is Al & this is John, I Pastor Greater Grace Chapel here in Lynchburg, so are you connected (use this word, not are you a part of, connected is specific, it means committed and you will get a more honest answer as I usually do) to a local Church?"* I like this question for a few reasons, one is because it often leads to good conversations, for instance if they say no, then I will ask *"why is that?"* and depending upon their answer we are off to the races so to speak. Their answer allows us to go down a few different roads depending upon why they do not or stopped attending a Church. Also if they say yes, I'll always ask where they attend and the name of the Church because sometimes I'll hear well I am a member of Jehovah's Witnesses or perhaps they will say I am a Latter Day Saint *(Mormon)* and again we are off to the races, so another important equipping factor is to be sure you know a lot about those two pseudo-Christian sects and have done some good study on them before beginning your door to door ministry as you will undoubtedly run into a few of them in your travels and being equipped will allow you to talk effectively and intelligently with them. I have a family at GGC who were once Mormon and it was my probing honest and direct questions that finally broke through which allowed them *(in tandem with the Holy Spirit of course)* to see the truth and come to Christ.

- ## **Proper Dress**

Dress neat casual, jeans and a button down shirt are fine, but always stay away from a suit and tie, this will give the outward appearance of being JW's or if you wear white shirts with black pants and a black tie you will look like a Mormon. I have often had people say they knew I wasn't either of those due to my casual dress so this is a very important point to remember. Also, please don't bring a briefcase; again you will look like a JW, so just have your little notebook, pen, cards, flyers and compact Bible in your back pocket and you will be fine.

- ## **Do Not Open Carry Your Bible!**

Now this may upset a few of you, but God's word tells us this in Matthew 10:16 (HCSB) *"Look, I'm sending you out like sheep among wolves. Therefore be as shrewd as serpents and as harmless as doves".* Be wise! Bible's scare people, especially big Bible's! If you want to bring a Bible, as I mentioned above get yourself a compact New Testament and keep it in your coat or back pocket. As you've read in chapter 8 I choose to *"hide God's word in my heart".* This is due *to* learning a real lesson a few years back when I was carrying my Bible with me, people were far more hostile, now granted this was New England, but I did notice quite a change when I began to carry a compact edition instead in my back pocket. So as I shared with you earlier I can go to any of those 25 verses at any time as well as many others I have taken the time to learn by heart so I can reference them by heart at almost anytime, anywhere, please do the same. And last, when I quote Scripture which I often do, I take a moment to tell whomever I'm speaking to that I am not quoting Scripture to sound knowledgeable or to show off, I am doing it because I want the hearer to know what God says, not me!

- **Stay Away From Christianese**

I addressed this problem in chapter 9. *"Christianese"* is a coded language we speak among believers that unbelievers often do not understand. This is very true when you are at someone's door who is not a Christian. Please refer back to chapter nine and the words I singled out not to use without framing them propcrly. We want to be effective communicators; using Christianese really takes away from that effectiveness. Often time's people are left wondering or are uncertain what we are saying and here's the dangerous part, 90% of the time the listener won't stop to ask you what you mean! It's sort of like when I was in sales there was a deadly truth that was almost never given attention to and it was this: 95%

of the people who never buy from you again will ever tell you why unless you ask! In all my time in sales on both on the road and in the office I can only recall 1 time, yep that's right, one time that a customer called me to tell me why he wasn't going to use our Company again! And my conservative estimate over my 20+ years in the building materials industry was that I was involved in some manner with over 35 million worth of sales. That's a statistic we better pay attention to! In like manner, a high percentage of those who hear those Christianese words won't ask you what they mean so **DON'T** use them please!

- **Probe And Be Bold**

In Matthew 7:7 Jesus said *"Keep asking, and it will be given to you. Keep searching, and you will find. Keep knocking, and the door will be opened to you"*. Nowhere is this more true than going door to door and I'll explain. First let's talk about probing. Ask direct questions, don't be afraid as people will appreciate and respect you more if you are direct and straightforward, pulling no punches so to speak. This type of ministry is not for the shy or timid! You will never get the information you need if you don't probe and probe effectively. The better the question, the better the answer that will be given which in turn will help you *"size up"* where that person is in their spirituality, etc. Second is to be bold. Ask them for personal contact information, email, cell FB info, etc. These are fantastic ways in today's world to stay in touch with them. I can't tell you how many have started looking at my Facebook page and came to the realization as one person put it by saying that I was the *"real deal",* a true compliment in today's society and its hostile outlook upon Ministers of the Gospel. As far as I am concerned, the more ways I have to stay in touch with a person, the better!

Last, the reason I said that Matthew 7:7 applies well here is because no matter what type of day you may be having just keep knocking and witnessing in whatever manner you are that day friends and eventually you will come to the right door, it never fails for those who **DO NOT** give up, especially after a tough encounter, after all, isn't getting knocked down only to jump back who we are called to be? I can't tell you how many times when I've not given up after a tough encounter the Lord has blessed me with an unforgettable encounter and He will do the same for you!

And allow me to give you this most important last thought about going door to door or about having a set time to reach out in whatever manner. It never ceases to amaze me that on the days I **DO NOT** wake up feeling well or for whatever reason don't have the heart or desire to go that morning *(just being* *honest)* I quickly learned to expect that God was going to do something fantastic that day and trust me when I say, He almost always did, so don't allow that to hold you back. Some of the most powerful times I've had in the field where on day's I almost didn't go! In fact, just last year a man I lead to the Lord some 6 years ago passed away from cancer. His life was drastically changed the day I walked up his driveway with my friend Mike. And because of that day, he is now home with Jesus. I shudder to think of those many times I wanted to stay home and where those folks might be today. That's not to say that God couldn't reach them without me, but as I have already made very clear, He uses people friends!

Chapter 14

Evangelism and Church Planting

Ok so what is the connection here? Well here is my thinking on this. Many Church planters rarely start by thinking about evangelizing their local area. I have been in many, many Church planting meetings and have rarely heard anyone talk about local Evangelization. It's almost always about the *"launch team"* and while that is very important, I think that getting some *"boots on the ground"* early is equally as important and that is where I think some launches end up failing as there is little or no connection to the local populace ahead of time. And one of those ways to get the word out is to begin a door to door campaign in advance. I'd recommend about 90 days out. It will also give you a good *"pulse"* on the local community, where they are and what their thinking is spiritually. In fact, my recommendation is that you not only start this campaign some 90 days out, but you keep it going on a continuous basis recognizing that it can be an effective tool to reach people and of course we know that God always blesses obedience to His word and we are helping to fulfil Matthew 28:19 via the door to door ministry and other witnessing opportunities.

And one of the best things I love about going door to door is this. Because I'm a Pastor, it is far too easy for me to lose a connection with the *"outside"* world living in a sort of *"Church World Bubble"*, so going door to door helps me to keep my hand on the pulse of the local *"Joe or Mary"*. What their concerns are, what they are thinking, feeling and going through in the toil of daily living, etc. So there are many advantages to keeping a record of what the locals are telling you! Less intrusive, but also yielding less information is going around to places like Walmart or any *"big box"* and just perusing the parking lot and doing mainly hand out's which I covered in chapter 12. Of course there are also things like local mailings which will certainly give you more bang for your buck, but it's nowhere near as personal as the other two ways are. I've always put a high premium on the personal way. I love getting in front of folks, nothing is quite like it. So while this is a short chapter, I hope these few pages are found to be helpful.

Chapter 15

Final Thoughts / About the Author / Endorsements

Rev. Al Stewart, D.D.

Currently makes his home in Forest, VA. with his wife Dawn. He has 2 sons as well as a stepson. Al has pastored for over 26+ years and is currently the Senior Pastor of Greater Grace Chapel in Lynchburg, VA. *(greatergracechapel.com)* He is a native of Waterbury, Ct. and attended Golden State School of Theology and

Schofield Seminary later earning an Honorary Doctorate from Adonai International Christian University *[A.I.C.U.]* for his Apologetics work among Jehovah's Witnesses and Latter Day Saints. Pastor Al is also an ordained Police/Fire Chaplain through Shield of Faith Ministries and is ordained through Adonai International Fellowship Alliance *[A.I.F.A.]* and serves as Asst. Chaplain of the Post 16, American Legion of Lynchburg, Va. He served in the U.S. Army from 1977-80 in West Germany. He has appeared on TBN's *"Praise the Lord"* program as well as many other broadcasts and is available on occasion to speak. Pastor Al can be reached at the address and email below. For additional copies of this or any of the following books at a discounted price please write:

PoBoy Publishing
PO Box 622
Forest, Va. 24551 *(email: rev.stuw@yahoo.com)*

Additional Books Available by Rev. Al Stewart through PoBoy Publishing:

"Works Revisited" (Amazon/KDP)

"Mormonism Revisited" (Amazon/KDP)

"The Watchtower Revisited, Dangerous Doctrines of Jehovah's Witnesses" (Amazon/KDP)

"The Importance of Just One Revisited" (Amazon/KDP)

"Put Your Hands Up" (An arrest warrant from God) Author: Officer Bob Faubel, Ret.

© 2019

What Is Being Said About This Book

"For those who might need encouragement to witness, this could be your book. Many books may have been written on this subject; however Al Stewart knows how from the experience of doing what he writes".

- *Rev. Bud Crawford*

Founding pastor of All Peoples Church - Lynchburg, VA

"Truth is best communicated in the realms of an interpersonal and conversational approach. Al Stewart's background in sales provides a wealth of experience on how to share the gospel in a casual, non-threatening and winsome way. Evangelism should be the natural flow of every Christian's conversation. Al has done a masterful job in providing the biblical foundation of evangelism along with the personal,

practical tips that help the Christian recover the confidence needed to effectively communicate the Gospel message in our 21st century multicultural communities. This refreshing book includes personal insights, real-life illustrations and interesting strategies that will encourage the believer to share the timeless message of the gospel in culturally relevant ways. Pastor Stewart's book "Sharing Jesus Effectively" will leave you seeking opportunities to share the "Good News".

- Dr. Randy Spencer

Director of Church Revitalization, Rawlings School of Divinity, Liberty University

57855282R00095

Made in the USA
Columbia, SC
15 May 2019